# OFFICE SPACE

## THE BOOK

# OFFICE SPACE

## THE BOOK

**How to Achieve the Best Office Space Opportunity Available**

# BARRY BASS

BARRYBASS@OUTLOOK.COM
CELL: 847-302-4894

**Office Space**
**The Book**

*iUniverse books may be ordered through booksellers or by contacting:*

*iUniverse*
*1663 Liberty Drive*
*Bloomington, IN 47403*
*www.iuniverse.com*
*1-800-Authors (1-800-288-4677)*

*ISBN: 978-1-4759-7851-3 (sc)*
*ISBN: 978-1-4759-7850-6 (e)*

*Print information available on the last page.*

*iUniverse rev. date: 11/08/2018*

**What You Will Find in This Book**

**Introduction**

How you will benefit by reading this book

Qualifications of the expert office leasing professional

**How to identify your office space needs**

**Negotiating the cost of office space**

Financial considerations

**Bass office space computer analysis**

A sophisticated analysis of leasing alternatives

**Where to locate your office**

**Achieving flexibility and growth opportunities**

Keeping your options open

**How to negotiate a fair lease document**

Negotiating leasing terms

**Which office building features are important to you**

Office building features and characteristics

**Getting what you want in constructing your office**

Work letter and tenant construction

**Office space professionals**

What other services are needed in relocating your office

**Bass occupancy cost analysis**

Bass lease abstract form

How to keep track of complicated lease terminology

# A Word about Barry J. Bass

Barry J. Bass, founder of Bass Consulting takes the pain out of the costly and complex business of office leasing. For decades, Chicago area tenants and owners alike have sought out his experience and real estate savvy to find the best opportunity and fit for their needs.

With strong, long standing relationships in the real estate brokerage community, Mr. Bass has leased over 10 million square feet of office space and negotiated the signing of more than 1000 leases in Chicago and the surrounding area.

Barry J. Bass possesses unparalleled success as owner/developer in-house and director of leasing for major high rise office buildings. He played a central role in securing the land assemblage for 120,000 square feet of the most iconic property in Chicago, the Willis Tower, formerly, the Sears Tower.

He provides expert consulting in buying and selling of income property. Barry J. Bass is skilled at financial analysis and projections, mortgage loan negotiation, project marketing and leasing, negotiation of lease documents.

Author of the recently released Office ***Space: The Book***, Mr. Bass provides an insightful glimpse into the world of income property. ***Office Space: The Book*** is filled with the valuable information every prospective tenant must know before looking for new space or signing a lease agreement.

A lifelong Chicago area resident and business owner, Mr. Bass is committed to helping business thrive in this great region.

Leasing office space is costly and complex. You should have the knowledge and right people at your side. Award winning, licensed and highly sought after, Barry J. Bass expertly guides sellers and buyers to the best fit possible.

# Qualifications of the Expert Office Leasing Consultant

1. **Experience**

   a. Length of time in business; continuing education
   b. Record of success, list clients as references to contact
   c. Hundreds of leases negotiated

2. **Knowledgeable**

   a. Tenant space analysis—physical & economic
   b. Lease document analysis & negotiation
   c. Total office space market at that time
   d. Available building opportunities
   e. Keep up to date
   f. Sublease opportunities
   g. Office building financing methods
   h. Operating expenses & real estate taxes

3. **Financial capabilities**

   a. Computer projection costs
   b. Preparation of proposal requests from landlords
   c. Comparative analysis of proposals
   d. Creation of alternative financial proposals

4. **Negotiation background**

   a. Relationships with building and leasing agents
   b. Comparative leases in market
   c. Proven ability to obtain tenants objectives
   d. Determine reasonable alternatives
   e. Significant stature in office space community

# How to Identify Your Office Space Needs

A complete review of your present office space situation should be done on an annual basis. When you are up-to-date on your office space you are better prepared to act if a change in your company or an advantageous leasing opportunity arises.

Is your present space adequate? How do your present occupancy cost relate to market conditions? Are there options in your lease that allow you to enlarge or consolidate your space or to renew or cancel your lease? Is your present situation the best it can be? Use the chart on the next page to always know your occupancy cost. Do this annually so you are up to date.

## Unique Charts Keep You Informed

As in most business situations, information is the key to making proper decisions. A 40 to 50 page lease document doesn't easily lend itself to scrutiny so we have developed the Lease Abstract Form. This form should be completed immediately before your lease is executed. It contains space for all necessary information about your lease and the interpretations of various clauses. If a problem arises, the Lease Abstract Form will save you time and provide you with the right information.

The second chart is an Occupancy Analysis form. This chart is to be completed on a monthly and annual basis. When this chart is kept up to date, you will always be aware of your office space costs.

You will find copies of this valuable form on the following page.

The following page will provide you with the information which will help you analyze your present situation and determine if a change should be made.

# Bass Occupancy Cost Analysis Form

The Occupancy Cost Analysis charts provide an easy way to track the costs of your office space. Using them to record occupancy costs on a monthly basis keeps you up-to-date on your office space economics. A once-over glance tells you how your office costs relate to your budget and also to market rentals.

Below, you will find this form. Gather and complete the information. You now have your true cost for the space. Complete the first column then replicate the form for a full lease period. Once this is done you should have a leasing specialist look it over and compare it to what can be found in the market place.

## Bass Occupancy Cost Analysis Form

1.  Base Rent Gross or Net                                   $_____
2.  Escalation Over Base                                     $_____
3.  Real Estate Tax Gross or Net                             $_____
4.  Escalation Over Base                                     $_____
5.  Operating Expense Gross or Net                           $_____
6.  Escalation Over Base                                     $_____
7.  CPI Expense Protects Owner's Equity                      $_____
8.  Escalation Over base                                     $_____
9.  Rent Concessions (free rent, furniture, etc.)            $_____
10. Electricity                                              $_____
11. Water                                                    $_____
12. Gas                                                      $_____
13. Cleaning                                                 $_____
14. Other Maintenance                                        $_____
15. After Hours Cooling/Heating                              $_____
16. Freight Elevator Changes                                 $_____
17. Office Insurance                                         $_____
18  Improvements Amortization (If Tenant pays)               $_____
19. Other Lump Sum Amortization                             $_____
20. Parking (if applicable)                                  $_____
21. Misc. Related Expenses                                   $_____
22. Total Occupancy Cost                                     $_____
23. Occupancy Cost usable per sq. ft.                        $_____
    (divide line 22 by usable sq. ft.)
24. Occupancy Rentable per sq. ft.                           $_____
    (divide line 22 by rentable sq. ft.)

USABLE SQ. FT. _____ RENTABLE SQ. FT. _____

# How to Identify Your Office Space Needs

## A. Economic

1. What is your total occupancy cost
   a. Rent
   b. Tax escalation
   c. Operating expense escalation
   d. CPI increases
   e. Electrical costs
   f. Repairs & maintenance
   g. BASS OCCUPANCY COST ANALYSIS (See page 6)

2. Opportunities in the office space market
   a. Tenant's market—abundance of space available (rent goes down)
   b. Landlords market—very low vacancy rates (rent goes up)
   c. Subleasing market
   d. Alternative buildings in your rental range
   e. Tax laws
   f. Other opportunities available

## B. Timing

1. How close is your lease to expiration
2. Review lease options
   a. Renewals
   b. Cancelation
   c. Expansion
   d. Contraction

3. Will present landlord negotiate your lease early
   a. Building present occupancy level
   b. Owner's desire to keep your tenancy long term
   c. Show owner this will be beneficial for him

## C. Quality of present space

1. Company growth
   a. More space required
   b. Less space required
   c. Different configuration required

2. Space no longer reflects proper image
3. Limited use of high tech equipment

4. Employment problems
   a. Absenteeism & turnover increasing
   b. Competitors attracting better employees

## D. Quality of present building

1. No longer reflects proper image for your company
2. Change of ownership or managing agent
   a. Not responsive
   b. Reduction in services
   c. Operating expenses increasing

3. Problems with building systems
4. Age of building or present build-out
5. Change in quality of tenants
6. Does not have ability to keep up with technology

## E. Location

1. Present location no longer advantageous
2. Additional locations required
3. Consolidation of various locations for economics
   a. Within building
   b. Within geographical area

Remember, this book is valid no matter what class the building is in because you will be comparing the same class of buildings that fit the budget of the client.

## Negotiating the Cost of Office Space

Just how much a company has to pay for the space it needs over a period of time is an important factor in a lease agreement. For some, rent per square foot is the key element in lease negotiations. We believe there are a number of other factors that impact on total occupancy cost just as much as rent per square foot.

Among the most important elements of obtaining an advantageous lease are timing, setting realistic objectives, understanding present market conditions and creation of a total economic package. Actually, how open a landlord is to negotiating depends on the state of the present office space market, the size of the tenant's need and the complexity of tenant improvements.

Timing is a prime factor. Knowledgeable tenants review their office space situation annually to take advantage of opportunities when they arise.

**There Are Negotiable Conditions & Dollar Judgments in Every Paragraph of the Lease.** Many of these dollars are real costs today. Others are potential costs of opportunities tomorrow. We can identify these costs and create alternative financial concepts to best utilize these dollars. Because we have represented major office building developments we understand the financing arrangements, are totally aware of the market and the needs of both tenant and building owner.

If net present dollars are important to a tenant today, we can make changes and shift higher dollar payments to later years. If a cash flow problem exists the payment of the rent can be adjusted to allow the tenant to build up cash reserves. There are various techniques to accomplish almost any need. The only limiting factor is the creativity of the parties involved.

A successful negotiation assures the building owner that the proposed arrangement will work for him. How the owner of an office building comes to a decision on money matters depends on the make-up of the owning entity and the financing package he obtained and is under obligation to operate. There are many items that have different values to different types of owners and even these values change as the building goes through its life cycle.

The computer analysis we use to study comparative leasing arrangements includes assumption based on our knowledge and experience. Examples of our computer generated lease analysis are contained in another section of this book. This analysis shows pure dollars projected to be spent over the life of the lease basis and per square foot. In instances there are notable differences between various proposals to be more or less than the others. Based on the analysis of initial proposals, discussions with our client and budget criterion we create a new proposal for each building under consideration. Theses are then presented to the various building owners to see if they can remain competitive.

The detailed Financial Considerations, outlined on the following pages, describe most of the pure dollar items that affect the cost of office space. Many of these items are not found anywhere in the lease document and are only brought to light by use of an experienced expert leasing consultant. Many times at best and final is given by either party and will actually take the highest or lowest as the case may be.

# Financial Considerations

### A. Rent

1. Amount
2. Method of payment
   a. Level of payment—the same amount of base rent is paid each month during the life of the lease
   b. Stepped schedule—once the rental rate for the term is negotiated it can be adjusted so that lower payments are made in the beginning and higher payments are made in the later years or vise versa
   c. Rent buy down—This is method used to combine the value of a rent concession period with the compounding of interest to create a lower but level rent payment plan
   d. Prepayments & lump sums—depending on the financial condition and tax positions of both the tenant and landlord this might be used to gain a lower effective rental rate and depends on the use and cost of money
   e. Creative alternatives

3. Items included in rent
   a. All operating expenses and taxes—gross lease
   b. No operating expenses and taxes—pure net lease
   c. Some combination of net & gross

4. Definition of rent—what types of payments of money are considered rent & how does this affect default provisions. Separate the obligation to and only the following are considered to be rent payment of "rent" and all other payments so if a default occurs it is not a major event.

### B. Rent concessions

1. Any period of rent abatement—free rent period
   a. When
   b. Is concession on gross or net rent

2. Equity participation—in exchange for signing a lease at market rentals some tenants have received an equity (ownership) position in the entire building. This only occurs when the tenant takes a major portion of the building and under certain circumstances.
   a. What is the real value of the equity
   b. What are the tax implications
   c. What are the risks (and there are risks)
   d. Does this work for the tenants best interest
   e. Who gets the equity
   f. What happens if the tenant moves
   g. Is an investment required

      h.    Other—this concept does not work to the best interest of most tenants. Upon full analysis it is usually better to take the concession package offered. There are many implications involved which require careful consideration.

   3.    Equity replacement—similar to above but actual ownership is not obtained

## C.  Additional concessions

1. Cash
2. Moving expenses
3. Telephone system
4. Additional tenant improvements
5. Lease assumptions
6 Promise of future business

## D.  Expense escalations

1.    Taxes—real estate & other
    a.    Base year, tax stop or net method
    b.    Is tax amount realistic
    c.    Is building fully assessed
    d.    Projection of future increases
    e.    Will landlord cap future increases
    f.    When is next quadrennial or reassessment
    g.    Gross up provision—see vocabulary
    h.    Cash or accrual method used
    i.    Other applicable taxes—lease tax, head tax, future tax is not known at present, either replacement or other.
    j.    What taxes are omitted—income tax, personal property, etc.

2.    Building operation expenses
    a.    Base year, stop or net method
    b.    Is base amount realistic
    c.    What expenses are included—get list
    d.    What expenses should be omitted
    e.    Treatment of building management expenses—personnel included—all beneath the building manager
    f.    Treatment of capital expenditures & definition example
    g.    Treatment of cost saving devices—if actual savings can be escalated, included
    h.    Building expense history—5 years
    i.    Projection of future increases
    j.    Will landlord cap future increases

# Financial Considerations (cont.)

3. Payment
   a. Lump sum at end of year
   b. Estimated payments made throughout the year
   c. Caps on estimates

## E. Rent escalations

1. Are there any increases in rent & when
2. Specific amounts or percentages
3. Increases based on consumer price index (CPI)
   a. Which index is used—national, regional, city
   b. What happens if index is no longer published
   c. How is base determined
   d. What percentage of rent is subject to increase
   e. How often are increases applied
   f. When do they commence

4. Can these increases be capped
5. Are increases compounded
6. Are increases cumulative
7. Are increases on gross or net rent
8. Should be on equity invested only as the expense side is escalated automatically by price increases on expense items

## F. Space measurement

1. How are "rentable" areas measured
2. How are "usable" areas measured—what is add on factor
3. Are all tenants on same method
4. How does this affect your occupancy cost—can be significant

## G. Financial impact analysis of lease arrangement

1. How is your cash flow affected
2. Long & short term affect on balance sheet
3. Tax implications
4. Computer analysis of alternatives
   a. Projected cost over term
   b. Net present value of each alternative
   c. Shows different values for various financial alternatives
   d. Tenant growth pattern

## H. Other

1. Are any other potential costs identified
2. Who pays for cleaning
3. Who pays for electricity

## I. Implications to landlord

1. Understanding of needs—both tenant & landlord
2. Compromise positions
3. Marketplace conditions—Will dictate rent negotiations

## J. Leasing versus owning—many tenants at some point consider owning a building instead of leasing space. This decision requires careful consideration to both the benefits received and the risks inherited with property ownership.

1. Cash investment required—becomes Non Liquid funds on balance sheet
2. Tax implications for owner, owner's corporation, and partners
3. Size of building
   a. Will it provide for expansion
   b. Risk and cost of vacant space

4. Subjective values
   a. Prestige
   b. Location
   c. Signage

5. Responsibility being a landlord
6. Owning entity—personnel, partnership, LLC, etc.
7. Analysis—complete financial analysis must be done comparing ownership to leasing.
8. Tax amplifications
9. Capital required for repairs & maintenance. A complete physical inspection must be done
10. Condominium—Difference of ownership
11. Co-op form of ownership is mostly found in residential situations. All occupants are owners of the property and are all responsible for the entire mortgage. This is very risky because if one owner drops out the remaining owners are still responsible for the entire mortgage.

# Bass Office Space Computer Analysis

Our computer analysis program gives our tenant clients the opportunity to comparatively shop leasing alternatives.

Most building owners today make complicated economic arrangements to finance their projects. Changing tax structures and week market conditions can compound their situation.

The proposals they offer tenants are based on their particular needs. The different economic features of each proposal have a decided impact on the total lease tern economics.

Though one building has a rental rate of $20 per square foot per year compared to another at $22, the lower base rent may not actually offer the best leasing opportunity for the tenant. Base rent per square foot is but one item that makes up the total occupancy cost of a lease.

The Bass Computer Analysis considers all possible economic components in a proposed lease. It provides n estimate of the total costs for the entire term. These estimates are on both total dollar and net present value basis. We then transfer these various estimates to a comparison chart so our client can easily compare the proposals offered by various landlords.

The value of a Bass Computer Analysis is twofold:

> It provides answers as to the cost of each alternative.

> It provides a basis for continuing negotiation.

Suppose a tenant likes Buildings A, B, and C & D. Building A would actually be preferred if the costs were the same or even slightly higher. The Bass Computer Analysis reveals exactly what area (rent, basement, CPI, etc) is causing Building A to be higher than competitive buildings. It provides the basis for us to discuss what area Building A can alter to make the building more feasible for our client. Applying this information, we create alternative proposals for the ownership of Building A to consider which can give both the client and the owner what they need.

The following computer analysis for four buildings reveals how a building with a higher rental rate actually offers a tenant a better leasing opportunity.

# Where to Locate Your Business

The oldest axiom in the real estate business is LOCATION, LOCATION, LOCATION. As far as location deals with the subject of office space, I have found that it is one of the most subjective decisions that a company has to make. The decision making process on where to locate ranges from very sophisticates studies dealing with where employees live, what modes of transportation they take, proximity to various important clients, services and etc. to the simple fact that the chief executive wants to walk to work. Location decisions are, for the most part, made by the highest ranking executive in the particular office that is contemplating a move. About the most objective aspect of location decisions is that it does have some economic impact on the cost of space.

Areas with a perceived prestige factor will determine higher rents. Buildings of the same quality located in different areas of the same city will have slightly different rental rates mostly because of a differential in the cost land, demand for space in that area and the prestige factor.

Certain, businesses do have locational boundaries and decisions as to the exact building are the only ones open to discussion. Most major law firms and banks are located in the central core of a metropolitan area. Regional corporate offices can be in the central city or any of the various suburban office zones.

One fact that has had an impact on the old traditional location values is the high degree of technology in telecommunications and data transmissions available today. Most decisions today are made for the convenience of the human need or desire to be close to something or to avail oneself of a certain prestige factor.

# Locating Your Office

## A. Geographical area

1. Which state
2. Which city
   a. Urban
   b. Suburban
   c. Rural

## B. Factors to consider

1. Availability of proper labor pool
2. Importance of various forms of transportation
3. Political climate
4. Zoning and building codes
5. Tax structure
   a. Corporate taxes
   b. Individual taxes
   c. Personal property tax
   d. Lease taxes
   e. Employee "head" taxes—sales tax
   f. Other

6. Legal structure or legislative environment

## C. Location of building

1. Proximity to firms you do business with
2. Proximity to area amenities
   a. Restaurants
   b. Shopping
   c. Courts & government offices
   d. Financial services—banks, exchanges
   e. Private clubs—health, social, business

3. Transportation
   a. Public transportations
   b. Commuter train stations
   c. Access to major highways
   d. Access to airports, train & bus depots

3. Prestige
   a. Building address
   b. Building Name
   c. Prestigious other tenants
   d. Tenants who are competitors

## D. Location within building

1. Which floor
2. Prestige factor
3. View
4. Adjacent tenants
5. Ability to expand
6. Signage

# Achieving Flexibility & Growth Opportunities

This section deals with the vitality of your company. In times past when short term leases (one to five years) were what both tenant and landlord wanted, flexibility was easier to accomplish. Today this is not the case. Lease terms of five to twenty years are a must for both tenant and landlord. While longer terms leases are a positive they can also be so limiting that they can affect the financial well being of a company.

Most leases should be structured with various options. These options will allow the company flexibility and alternative choices during the term of the lease dependent upon the direction of the corporate growth. Some options can be easily obtained while others are more difficult. A review of the various options should be made and those determined to be important should be obtained even if a cost is attached thereto. Usually, the options having a cost will only have the cost if the option is exercised. In most instances if a company finds its self in a situation where the option must be exercised the cost attached thereto will usually be worthwhile. I have been involved in numerous situations where huge sums of money were paid to landlords, during the term of the lease, to obtain various rights due to a change in corporate growth. In most instances these rights would have been granted for little or no cost if negotiated when the lease was signed. Of course, obtaining options does depend on the state of the office market at the time the lease is being negotiated.

These options are so important to certain businesses that I have put them in a separate section so that they get the consideration necessary.

## A. Length of Lease

1.     Options to renew
   a.     How many & length of each
   b.     At what rental
   c.     Length of notice required
   d.     What will building provide—repaint, etc.

2.     Option to cancel
   a.     When
   b.     Length of notice
   c.     What penalty

## B. Options for expansion space

1.     Rights of first offer
2.     Rights of first refusal
3.     Specific amounts of space at specific times
4.     What rental rate
5.     What improvements
6.     Length of notice

## C. Option to contract space

1.     When
2.     How much apace
3.     Penalty
4.     Length of notice

## D. Subleasing & assignment provisions—This is also a lease provision which requires careful consideration

1.     With or without landlord's permission
2.     Recapture clause
3.     All or part of the space
4.     All or part of the term
5.     Who keeps the profit, if any
6.     Definition of profit
7.     Notice provision
8.     Continuing liability of prime tenant
9.     Conformity with use clause
10.    Related corporate entities

**E. Transfer of tenants interest**

1. Sale of business
2. Changes in stockholders equity
3. Security deposit
4. Bankruptcy by either tenant or owner or lender

**F. Option to purchase**—There are instances if the tenant is sizeable enough and intends to expand in the building over time that it may be advantageous to own the building.

1. When can the option be exercised
   a. Certain date in the future
   b. When the tenant attains a certain occupancy percentage of the building
   c. Right of first refusal or first offer if another bona fide offer is presented
   d. Multiple and various items

2. At what price
   a. Predetermined specific price
   b. Formula based on capitalization rates
   c. Formula based on market rate determination

3. Reasons for purchase
   a. Economics
   b. To prevent adverse situation during tenancy

# How to Negotiate a Fair Lease Document

The lease document is the agreement between tenant and landlord which will affect the quality of life for the tenant for the entire lease term. Most leases have two qualities which are the same no matter where the office space is located;

1.   They are complex
2.   They are landlord oriented

There are at least three people who should review the lease:

1.   An executive of the tenant
2.   A qualified leasing consultant
3.   A competent real estate lawyer for legal advice only

I cannot stress strongly enough that the lawyer chosen should be totally familiar with real estate and lease law. I have negotiated many leases with corporate lawyers who do not understand the intricate concepts or acceptable language of various lease clauses. When this happens either items that should be changed are not or the lawyer overcompensates by making so many changes that he puts the negotiation in jeopardy.

As Bass Consultants we do more than negotiate the economic terms. We also have sufficient knowledge to aid in negotiation of the lease document. This knowledge comes in the form of knowing what is common practice, what are the easy changes for most landlords, where are the subtle economic values in the lease and the fact that we have negotiated over 1,000 documents.

The lease document should be totally acceptable before it is signed. Although you may think the landlord is fair and a "nice guy" but when the going gets tough he will think about his rights before yours. Furthermore, buildings are sold and you may be faced with a new landlord with different operating procedures and the only rights you have are those contained in the lease. Although the lease is a legal document and the language seems precise there are instances where certain clause stated in a certain way will still be open to different interpretatios. When this happens over an important point, both parties will find themselves in court. When the lease is being negotiated and the point appears which may have different interpretations we have found that attaching an example in the form of a rider to the lease can be helpful.

After negotiating over 1,000 leases I still find new items to negotiate, different ways to look at the same thing and lawyers who bring up potential problems I have never heard before. The lease, no matter what attempt the landlord makes to simplify it is still a complex document and careful scrutiny and negotiation are necessary if it is to contain all the things that make it fortuitous for the tenant.

The items listed in the lease section that follows are by no means full and complete discussion but are included to point out most of the areas which greater care should be given during the negotiation. The most competent local real estate attorney you can find and afford should be retained for the negotiation. The items discussed in this section when combined with everything else in this book and when negotiated by competent people should provide the tenant with a situation that will not be limiting and in addition may provide opportunities in the future. These negotiations should be able to remove restrictive covenants which could be very costly if the goals of a company change during the life of the lease.

The lease should be fair for both tenant and landlord. If the tenant is so strong in the negotiation he may remove the incentive for the landlord to be a "nice guy". Although the lease gives the tenant certain legal rights a landlord who sits with the lease looking for a way to get even can cause the tenant problems and make his occupancy an unpleasant experience.

# Negotiating Lease terms

**A. Landlord's document is only a starting point, almost everything is subject to negotiation**

**B. Rent clause**

1.  What is definition of rent
2.  When is payment due
3.  Sufficient grace period is a must. After that a penalty may be assessed
4.  No default without written notice and notice of acceptance of notice

**C. Use clause**

1.  For what function you may use your office
2.  How you may use common areas of building
3.  Must be liberal enough to allow continued use of office if your business purpose changes
4.  If not liberal it may affect ability to sublease
5.  Any exclusives granted by landlord should not act to restrict tenant's use

**D. Building rules & regulations**

1.  Obtain list and be sure you initially comply & agree
2.  Additions should not act against normal operation of you business
3.  All rules & regulations should apply to all tenants equally
4.  If you are big enough try to get a favored nations clause

**E. Security deposit**

1.  Can this be waived
2.  Substitute for cash—letter of credit, etc.
3.  Returned if no default occurs within certain time period—2 years
4.  If cash is absolutely required obtain interest

**F. Casualty provision—if building or premises are damaged or destroyed**

1.  How long does landlord have to restore
2.  Can landlord cancel your lease & when
3.  Can you cancel your lease & when
4.  From when does your rent abate
5.  Whose insurance pays for what

# Negotiating Lease terms (cont.)

## G. Insurance

1. Type & amount required by landlord
2. What does landlord's insurance cover
3. What should your insurance cover—what limits, what insurance company and what rating
   a. Liability
   b. Casualty
   c. Business interruption

4. Subrogation features

## H. Transfer of tenants interest

1. What happens to lease if your business is sold
2. Can you restructure capital stock of your business without effectuating a defaults

## I. Default provisions

1. Upon default does entire rent become due
2. Differentiate between monetary & non-monetary
   a. Penalties should differ
   b. Time for cure should differ

3. Provision for written notice of default
4. Cure period after notice
5. Commence & diligent pursuit of cure should satisfy
6. Right if landlord defaults
   a. Cure period
   b. Tenant's right to cure & offset rent

## J. Holdover provisions—remaining after lease expires

1. Should not constitute a new lease
2. What is the rent for this property
3. Try to get from landlord a favored nations clause

## K. Non-disturbance attachments & agreements

1. Tenant's right to occupancy as long as no default
2. Obtain from owner and each lender
3. Vacating office—landlord's rights

**L. Relocation clause**—landlord's right to move your office to another but similar area of the building. Must be built out like original space, floor placement, elevator ID, view, etc. Tenant may choose to terminate lease if business is affected.

**M. Cancellation by landlord**

1. Demolition clause—If building is sold and the land may be more valuable than the building
2. Upon sale or transfer of owners interest

**N. After hours provisions**

1. What are building normal hours of operation
2. Do you have 24 hour access
3. After hours heating & cooling ability & cost

**O. Financial liability**

1. Is your business "corporate" signature sufficient
2. Personal liability
3. Limitation of personal liability
4. Security deposit required

**P. Waiver of claims**—do not waive landlords negligence

**Q. Landlord appointed attorney**—do not give up right to have your own attorney. No trial by jury is common

**R. Abandonment**

1. What happens if tenant moves during term of lease but continues to pay rent. If space is visible to outside, landlord may want to cancel the lease. Tenant may want to keep lease and not default as he may want space at later date.
2. Does entire term rental become due

**S. Enforceability**—Get same right as landlord including payment of attorneys fees to enforce tenants rights

**T. Reasonableness**—Tenant should try to obtain a general clause which states "When consent of landlord is required said consent shall not be unreasonably withheld or delayed". Landlord will want the right to cancel the lease, approve the sublease, recapture, and insist on any "profits" tenant negotiates.

U. **Subleasing & assignment**—discussed above under growth and flexibility. This clause can contain opportunities or restrictions and should be negotiated carefully.  Landlord may not want to be reasonable under certain situations involving safety & security of other tenants, payments of "rent" and other money issues.

# Which Office Building Features Are Important To You

What are the features that make a tenant choose to lease space in one building over another? Architectural style, materials used in the lobby or views from the building higher floors aesthetic considerations. The size and shape of the floor directly affects the amount of space required to house a company and therefore will effect the economics. Parking, building amenities, services available, restaurants and retail stores directly pertain to the needs of employees. While there are some differences, most new buildings are very similar in mechanical, fire safety, electrical and elevator systems.

At Bass & Co. we review exactly what characteristics are important to a client. Theses are them discussed with the client's space planner or architect to determine how each item may impact the client's budget.

Usually, the buildings with high grades for aesthetics and which contain an abundant amount of special features will cost more and therefore the rent will ne higher. The tenant must decide on which features are most important and then balance them against the cost of space.

# Office Building Features and Characteristics

## A. Building owner

    1.    Private or institutional owner
    2.    Experience & reputation

## B. Building Management

    1.    Owner managed or hired management firm
    2.    Experience & reputation
    3.    Comments from present tenants

## C. Available space

    1.    What floor
    2.    What area of the floor
    3.    What view
    4.    Who are the other tenants on that floor
    5.    Is your space option space for another tenant
    6.    Are there rental differences dependent on where in the building you locate
    7.    Identity

## D. Architectural style

## E. Building appearance

    1.    Type of facade
    2.    Type of windows
        a.    Color, tinted
        b.    Reflective ability
        c.    Single or double glazed

## F. Spatial considerations

    1.    Size of floor
        a.    Will you be a single floor tenant
        b.    Expansion space on same floor
        c.    Multi-floor occupancy is generally inefficient

    2.    Shape of floor
        a.    Distance between windows and core
        b.    Ratio of windows to interior space
        c.    Rectangular shape is usually most efficient

3. Module spacing (distance on exterior between windows) affects size of perimeter offices
4. Colum Spacing
   a. Number of columns per floor
   b. Bay size—distance between columns
   c. Colum free space
   d. Columns affect efficiency of interior space
   e. Wet columns (carry water to and waste lines to and from floor) important for sinks and toilets within the office space

5. Ceiling height
   a. Slab to slab
   b. To finished ceiling

## G. Lobby

1. Materials
2. Appearance
3. Staffing
   a. Security desk
   b. Level of security—cameras
   c. Identification of people going in & out

## H. Building Directory

1. Location, visibility & size
2. Access to visitors
3. Number of spaces available to tenants

## I. Restaurant & retail amenities

## J. Parking

1. Availability & adequacy for tenants & visitors
2. Covered or open
3. Cost
4. Cleanliness & security
5. Hours of operation
6. automated or Live attendants
7. level of lighting

### K. Storage availability

1. How much & where
2. Cost
3. Security, fire protection

### L. Building services or special features

1. Conference or meeting rooms
2. Library
3. Auditoriums
4. Vaults
5. Barber or beauty shop
6. Medical facilities
7. Messenger service
8. Health club
9. Access to major overnight delivery services
10. Bank or cash station
11. Secretarial or temporary help

### M. Elevatoring

1. Passenger elevators
   a. Total number in building
   b. Number in each bank of building
   c. Ratio to total sq. ft. in your section of building
   d. Transfer floor between sections of building
   e. Capacity of each car
   f. Attractiveness of car
   g. Durability of interior car materials
   h. Communications with security desk
   i. Is a transfer of cars necessary to reach office
   j. Visit building during peak operating hours and take elevator to proposed office
   k. Card reader availability—security
   l. Hours of operation

### N. Loading dock & freight elevator

1. Number & size of spaces
2. Truck access
3. Covered or open
4. Hours of operation

5. Freight elevators
   a. How many
   b. Weight capacity
   c. Inside measurements

## O. Security

1. Guards on duty at what times & where
2. Electronic surveillance
3. Card access systems or other—fingerprints
4. stairwell access

## P. Safety & emergency systems

1. Fire department command panel
2. Communications to tenants
3. Number of & access to stairwells
4. Sprinkler systems
5. Emergency generators
6. Smoke & fire alarms in space
7. Other building procedures

## Q. Public areas

1. Washrooms
   a. Space adequacy of facilities
   b. Location on floor
   c. Cleanliness
   d. Attractiveness
   e. Lounge in women's facility

2. Public drinking fountains
3. Provisions for the handicapped
4. Corridors, elevator lobbies

## R. Cleaning of office space

1. Is specification attached to lease
2. How often is each item done
3. What items are extra costs
   a. Carpet cleaning
   b. Lunchroom or kitchen
   c. Interior glass

4.    How often are exterior & interior windows washed

## S.  Mechanical systems

1.    Energy management & conservation systems
   a.    Does building have outside sensors, how many
   b.    Are there control devises on all systems
   c.    Are they computer controlled & monitored on a 24 hour basis

2.    age of system
3.    Is building using 100% of system capacity
4.    are there back-up boiler or air handlers
5.    Capacity of cooling tower
6.    Is system gas or electric fires
7.    Is system heat-by-light, electric resistance, forced air

## T.  Electrical system

1.    Capacity from utility company
2.    Transformer size
3.    Metering capability
4.    Capacity for each tenant—watts per sq. ft.
5.    Under floor system
6.    Raised floor through

## U.  Signage

1.    Policy of signage on tenant doors
2.    Signage availability for large tenant
   a.    Can building name be obtained
   b.    In building lobby
   c.    At or on roof
   d.    In elevators
   e.    In elevator lobby on tenant floors

# Getting What You Want In Constructing Your Office

The work letter & tenant construction documents pertain to how the office space will be constructed, the quality of items used and who bears the cost. The work letter is usually an attachment to the lease and is executed separately. Normally, after the space is constructed to the satisfaction of all concerned the work letter is of no consequences, unless it contains language referring to future alterations or latent defects.

There is room for negotiation in this document much the same as in the lease. The items of work contained in the work letter are the landlord's offer as to whether he will supply at his cost. This deals with both quantity and quality of items. After discussions with a space planner the tenant will have a better idea of what is needed to build the office space to the tenant's specifications. A space plan and a list of specification is then prepared and used as a basis of negotiation with the landlord, prior to lease being signed.

Office space market conditions and the balance if the economic lease terms will have the biggest affect on what is attainable in this area. Once the basic plans and specifications are determined the lowest cost if construction must be obtained or all the value that was gained in negation of the work letter can be given away by uncontrolled construction costs or high fees.

Competent advice from space planners is imperative to make the most of the construction budget obtained and to make sure that everything bargained for was received. When working with the space planner, alternatives for most items should be discussed as certain items which are totally acceptable can sometimes cost hale that which was initially specified. The tenant must determine what things are most important and that's where the emphasis should be.

When the space is to be built much consideration should be given to the contractors involved. They must be reputable and financially strong. If the owner of the building operates his own interior construction company they should be used if at all possible. If the owner builds the space he should stand by its quality. If something goes wrong he will fix it. If outside contractors are used and problems develop it could be more difficult to get that contractor to come back and do repairs once he has been paid, unless he does other work in the building.

## A. Plans

1. Who provides the space planner
2. Will landlord pay for the space planning
3. Who prepares, and pays for working drawings
4. Who gets & pays for construction permits
5. Are plan submission dates realistic & what happens if dates are not met

## B. Delays

1. What happens if a tenant caused delay occurs
2. What protection is given for landlord delays
3. Provisions for long lead time items

## C. Completion

1. Definition of substantial completion
2. Whose judgment
3. How & when is punch list performed
4. How are punch list item handled
   a. Punch list is items remaining to be completed even after tenant has moved

## D. Landlord's work

1. Quantity of items supplied by landlord
2. Quality of items
   a. Should have a date for completion or penalty kicks in

## E. Tenant's work

1. Additional items required to complete space
2. Will landlord supply & pay for these items
3. Is at tenant's cost will landlord par for these items and amortize over lease term
   a. Tax implications
   b. Who owns items
   c. Who gets items at end of lease term

## F. Economics

1. Is landlord the general contractor
2. Landlord markup—% added to cost of actual construction
3. Is landlord markup the same for landlord's work and tenant extra work

4. Are competitive bids obtained for all work
5. Will landlord convert construction items not used to a dollar allowance
6. Will landlord allow you to hire your own general or other contractors
   a. If so does landlord charge a supervisor fee and how much
   b. If so what is landlord's repair responsibility

## G. Building communications facilities

1. Major telephone company facilities
2. Private telecommunications
   a. Type of switch
   b. Capacity
   c. Limitations
   d. Services available
   e. Are costs competitive
   f. Wireless—servers

## H. Air-conditioning & heating system

1. type of system
2. Volume & velocity of air flow
3. Noise level caused by system
4. Space infringements
5. Number of temperature zones per floor
6. After hours capability & cost
7. Ability to add to system
8. Humidity control

## I. Lighting

1. Type of fixtures—building standard
2. Type of lighting
   a. Direct
   b. Indirect—value of reflective surfaces

3. Amount of fixtures supplied
4. Foot candles maintained at desktop
5. Quality of light—color
6. Who pay electric charge
7. Who pays & how much for tube or bulb replacement

## J. Electrical & telephone

1. Number of each type outlet supplied
2. Under floor duct system

3.   Conduit required
4.   Size of conduit supplied
5.   Who pays for electrical charges
6.   Who pays for meters
7.   Number of light switched provided
8.   Watts per sq. ft. available
9.   Capacity available for computers
10.  any special computer facilities, cooling, electrical

## K. Partitions

1.   Type of wall & stud
2.   Height—to ceiling of floor slab
3.   Acoustic qualities
4.   Insulation
5.   Amount supplied
6.   Fire rating
7.   Movable or not

## L. Doors

1.   Entrance
   a.   Type & material
   b.   Height
   c.   Security value
   d.   Amount supplied
   e.   Fire rating

2.   Interior
   a.   Type & material
   b.   Solid or hollow core
   c.   Height
   d.
   e.   Amount supplied
   f.   Fire rating

## M. Hardware

1.   Style & material
2.   Latch sets or lock sets
3.   Amount supplied
4.   Door closers

**N. Ceiling**

1.　Type of system
　　a.　Concealed grid
　　b.　Open grid
　　c.　Plaster

2.　Sound control ability
3.　Fire rating

**O. Floor & floor load**

1.　How many pounds per square foot
2.　Is it enough for computers & file rooms
3.　Who pays to increase load capacity
4.　Amount of deflection in floor
5.　Is concrete floor sealed

**P. Floor covering**

1.　type supplied by building
　　a.　Carpet or vinyl
　　b.　What grade colors

2.　Qualities
　　a.　Sound control
　　b.　Stain resistant
　　c.　Static electricity control

3.　Amount supplied by building

**Q. Window covering**

1.　Blinds, drape
2.　Amount supplied
3.　Match other tenants
4.　Tinted
5.　Other

**R. Painting & wall covering**

1.　Paint—how many coats
2.　How often will building repaint

3.     Color choice
4.     How many colors per room
5.     Availability of vinyl, paneling or other type

## S.  Acoustics

1.     What is acoustical quality of materials used
2.     Penetration of noise from outside or inside building

## Office Space Professionals

Professional guidance is available for each and every step involved in office relocation and much of it comes at no cost to the company making the move. Using professionals is the best way to insure that the acquisition and move to new office space is done in the proper manner and that the best opportunity is obtained at the least cost.

Barry J. Bass & Co. will provide the finest leasing consultation available. Other professionals required are space planners, communications consultants, computer consultants, commercial movers, a real estate lawyer, business machine consultants and possibly a management consultant.

An office move could provide your company with a wonderful opportunity, how good or bad the experience is up to you.

Barry J. Bass
Quality Tenant Representation
BARRYBASS@OUTLOOK.COM
847-302-4894

### A. Space Planner

1. Experienced—should have previously completed planning of a similar type office.

2. Same planner should do plans in all buildings under consideration.
   a. This should assure that all planning functions are done the same
   b. Requires less executives time in explaining requirements to many different planners

3. Planner & client determinations
   c. Number & size private offices
   d. Adjacency requirements of departments to each other & to other office facilities
   e. Adjacency requirements of people to other people
   f. Determination of location & size of all related facilities such as conference room, storage room, computer rooms, lunch rooms, libraries, mail room, typing pools, secretarial stations, etc.

4. Determination of location & amount of all construction items. This may include interior design functions such as quality, type & color of various items.
   c. Telephone outlets—sizing conduit, number
   d. Electrical service—placement of floor and wall outlets, duplex or quadplex, separate and dedicated circuits or data transmission.
   e. Wall switches—on-off, dimmers
   f. Walls—drywall, wood, glass, is insulation required, is blocking required to support weight of shelving, height of wall.
   g. Doors—height, solid or hollow core, paint grade, wood or metal frames
   h. Hardware—knob or lever, lockset or latch set, color, security locks
   i. Floor covering—carpet, vinyl, wood
   j. Window covering—blinds, drapes—must provide same look from outside
   k. Lighting fixtures—fluorescent, incandescent, wall washers, type of lenses, wattage of bulbs
   l. Ceiling—exposed grid, concealed grid, plaster
   m. Plumbing—private washrooms, sinks, drinking fountains, availability for additional air conditioning
   n. Special items or facilities—computers, data or word processing, projection equipment, food service, floor load capacities, etc.
   o. Wall covering—paint, wood, vinyl, etc.

5. Planner should review building standard construction items offered by landlord
    a. Are these items of sufficient quality to last the life of the lease
    b. Do they reflect the image the tenant wants
    c. Will building standard quantities be enough to construct the required facilities

6. Budget—Determine with tenant and tenant's broker how much will be obtained from the landlord
    a. If premises are not completely constructed & paid for by landlord (turkey construction) a budget must be determined which tenant can afford.
    b. Planner to give alternatives in achieving desired result using different levels of quality at various prices

7. Furniture plan
    a. Will furniture be moved
    b. Will new furniture be purchased
    c. Require to determine amount & location of telephone outlets, electrical outlets, CRT outlets, lighting fixtures

8. Tenant's requirement package
    a. Written list of all items including quantities & quality of each should be prepared
    b. Tenant space plan showing exact location of all construction items
    c. This package is then used by the office leasing broker in negotiations with the landlord

9. After lease signing
    a. Working drawings—whose responsibility & date of completion
    b. Supervision of work
    c. Determination of substantial completion
    d. Punch list supervision

## B. Communications consultant

1. Telephone system alternatives
2. Cost of installation
3. Cost of operation
4. Least cost routing availability
5. Number of lines required
6. Purchase of own switch

7. If owned can present switch be moved
8. Type & capability of switchboard
9. Type & capability of individual instruments
   a. Conferencing
   b. Speaker phones
   c. Paging & cell phones

10. Consultant to check capabilities of building
11. Data transmission capabilities
12. Expansion capabilities
13. Purchase or lease of equipment
14. Availability of billing broken down per each phone
15. Long distance carrier—analysis of which carrier will give best service for least cost
16. Experience, reputation, references
17. Up-to-date technology a must

## C. Computer and or business machines consultant

1. Experience, reputation, references
2. Utilize present or purchase of new computers
3. Capability of building to provide electrical capacity required
4. Floor load capacities
5. Air-conditioning
   a. Additional air-conditioning capabilities
   b. Hours air-conditioning required
   c. Cost for after hours air-conditioning

6. Minimizing interruption of service to make move

D. **Moving**—the actual is never easy. Interview various moving companies as choosing the proper one can minimize problems and provide systems to make the entire process easier

1. Experience, reputation & referrals of mover
2. Will you need to warehouse furniture of equipment
3. Actual packing should be done by each individual employee
4. Can provide opportunity to clean house, cull files
5. Provide mover with floor plans
6. All furniture and boxes should be coded as to where it goes in new space
7. Compare proposals of moving companies to determine number of people used, number of trucks used
8. Try to get a not to exceed price from mover

9. Tenant to have people at both ends of move to provide assistance and make sure nothing is damaged. Interview previous clients
10. As soon as actual date of move is determined contact both buildings to secure use of freight elevators
11. Determine with mover his claims policy
12. Determine with mover his insurance coverage

# Bass Occupancy Cost Analysis

The Occupancy Cost Analysis chart provides an easy way to track the costs of your office space. Using it to record occupancy costs on a monthly basis keeps you up-to-date on your office space economics. A once-over glance tells you how your office costs relate to your budget and also to market rental rates.

Our chart provides enough space to keep on complete list of costs. One copy of the chart will track expenses on monthly bases. Another copy will keep annual totals. The monthly chart facilitates annual accounting. Whether you are in the middle of a present lease or just beginning a new lease, why not complete them now.

I have provided the template which shows every expense your office has and that can be compared to other buildings or other locations your company has office space.

# Bass Lease Abstract

The BASS LEASE ABSTRACT is simply a synopsis of all the important points contained in the lease document. Today, most leases contain 25 pages or more of boilerplate language and in many instances attachments, riders and exhibits totaling another 5 to 10 pages, all of which is important. However, the BASS LEASE ABSTRACT will provide:

1.   An easy method of finding important information quickly.
2.   A method of translating legal lease language into simple English easily understood by most executives.
3.   An explanation of the concept behind a specific lease clause so that it is clear what the meaning is or why it was included.

Various lease clauses can have various interpretations. These interpretations can change each time the clause is read. This depends on who is doing the reading and the particular circumstances now present which is causing the specific reason to review the lease. The BASS LEASE ABSTRACT will help determine the original concepts and circumstances pertaining to that clause.

The BASS LEASE ABSTRACT form attached hereto provides space for the minimum amount of information to be provided. Additional pages can be attached containing the above mentioned explanations of various lease clauses.

# Bass Lease Abstract Form

Name of Building: _____

Building address: _____

_____

Name of tenant per lease: _____

_____

Name of landlord: _____

_____

Notices to landlord sent to: _____

_____

_____

_____

_____

_____

_____

Lease term: _____

_____

Sq. Ft. (rentable): _____

_____

Date of lease commencement: _____

_____

Date of lease expiration: _____

_____

Amount of base rent per sq, ft: _____

_____

    Monthly: _____

    Increases to base: _____

Date of rent payment: _____

_____

    Grace period: _____

Security deposit: _____

_____

    Date of return: _____

Lease guarantee: _____

_____

Rental concession (describe): _____

_____

_____

_____

Base year or stop for taxes: _____

    Cap (if any): _____

Base year or stop for expenses: _____

    Cap (if any): _____

Basis for CPI increases: _____
     Amount of increase: _____
     Cap (if any): _____
Additional costs: _____
_____
_____
_____

Expansion options: _____
_____
     Amount of space: _____
     Where located: _____
     Date of commencement: _____
     Date of notice: _____
     Rent: _____
     Construction: _____
Rights of refusal or offer: _____
_____
     Amount of space: _____
     Where located: _____
     Decision time after notice: _____
     Rent: _____
     Construction: _____
Termination: _____
_____
     Effective date: _____
     Notice date: _____
     Penalty: _____
Renewal option: _____
     How many: _____
     Length of each: _____
     Notice date: _____
     Rent: _____
     Construction: _____
Landlord right to cancel: _____
     Describe: _____
     Notice: _____
     Penalty: _____
Subleasing rights: _____
     Describe: _____
_____
_____
_____
     Approvals: _____
     Recapture: _____
     Profits: _____
     Notice: _____
     Exemptions: _____

Holdover provisions: _____
_____
Other: _____
_____
_____
_____
_____
_____
_____
_____
_____
_____
_____
_____
_____
_____
_____
_____
_____

## COMPARISON OF PROJECTED COSTS DATE: 9/8/2000 PAGE #

| ASSUMPTIONS | 123 MAIN STREET | 1100 OCEAN DRIVE | 7600 18TH STREET | PACIFIC PLAZA PLACE |
|---|---|---|---|---|
| COMMENCE | 11/1/2000 | 12/1/2000 | 1/1/2001 | 2/1/2001 |
| EXPIRATION | 12/31/2010 | 7/30/2011 | 8/31/2011 | 9/30/2011 |
| TERM | 10 YRS 2 MOS | 10 YRS 8 MOS | 10 YRS 8 MOS | 10 YRS 8 MOS |
| FLOOR | PART 16 | ENTIRE 12 | PART 23 | PART 4 |
| RENTABLE | 10,000 | 12,098 | 13,872 | 12,345 |
| LOSS FACTOR | 17.00% | 17.60% | 15.00% | 10.00% |
| USABLE AREA | 8,300 | 9,969 | 11,791 | 11,111 |
| ADD ON FACTOR | 1.20482 | 1.21359 | 1.17647 | 1.11111 |
| AVG BASE RENT | $24.07 | $27.25 | $27.25 | $25.50 |
| # MOS FREE RENT | 4.00 | 4.00 | 4.00 | 2.00 |
| $ VALUE FREE RENT | $6.67 | $8.67 | $8.67 | $4.17 |
| LL CASH CONTRIB | $25.00 | $20.00 | $17.00 | $13.50 |
| TENANT CASH | $15.00 | $10.00 | $6.00 | $6.50 |
| ELECTRIC $ | $3.00 | $2.75 | $2.50 | $1.50 |
| ELECTRIC INCREASE | 3.00% | 3.00% | | 2.00% |
| ESCALATION 1 | OPERATING | OPERATING | OPERATING | CAM |
| ESCALATION 1 BS YR | 2000 | 2001 | 2001 | 2001 |
| ESCALATION 2 | 3% PER ANNUM | 3% PER ANNUM | | CPI |
| ESCALATION 2 BS YR | 2000 | 2001 | | 2001 |
| R.E. TAX BASE YR | 2000 | NET COST | 2001.00 | 2001.00 |

| **TOTALS** | TENANT REP (PRE) | TENANT REP (PRE) | TENANT REP (PRE) | TENANT REP (PRE) |
|---|---|---|---|---|
| | DISC RATE = 8.00% | DISC RATE = 9.00% | DISC RATE = 9.00% | DISC RATE = 9.00% |
| TOTAL DOLLARS | $3,742,856 | $5,504,104 | $4,735,465 | $4,377,287 |
| PRESENT VALUE | $2,464,036 | $3,405,553 | $3,010,612 | $2,767,834 |
| AVERAGE COST P/A | $368,150 | $516,010 | $443,950 | $410,371 |
| NET EFFECTIVE P/A | $352,555 | $494,075 | $436,777 | $401.555 |
| RSF AVERAGE COST | $36.81 | $42.65 | $32.00 | $33.24 |
| RSF NET EFFCTV P/A | $35.26 | $40.84 | $31.49 | $32.53 |
| USF AVERAGE COST | $44.36 | $51.76 | $37.65 | $36.94 |
| USF NET EFFCTV P/A | $42.48 | $49.56 | $37.04 | $36.14 |

THE NET EFFECTIVE RATE PER ANNUM = THE PRESENT VALUE AMORTIZED OVER THE TERM AT THE DISCOUNT RATE SHOWN FOR EACH DEAL.

**OFFICE LEASING: THE BOOK**

**THE VOCABULARY OF LEASING OFFICE SPACE**

1.  **ADA**: Americans With Disabilities Act passed by Congress in 1994 with intent to provide persons with disabilities accommodations and access equal to or similar to that of the general public. Some considerations are ramps in addition to stairs, lowering of buttons in elevators, extra wide stall & rails in the restrooms, lever hardware throughout the building.

2.  **Additional Rent**: Any amounts due under a lease that are in addition to base rent. Most common form is operating expense increases.

3.  **Add-on-factor**: The ratio of rentable to useable square feet. Also known as the load factor and the rentable-to-usable ratio.

4.  **Allowance**: A set dollar amount provided by the Landlord under a lease to be used by the Tenant for a specific purpose. Examples include allowances for tenant improvements, moving expenses, design fees, etc. If the expense exceeds the allowance amount, such excess is the Tenant's responsibility. If the expense is less than the allowance, the savings are retained by the Landlord unless their agreement specifies otherwise.

5.  **Amortization**: Payment of debt in regular, periodic installments of principal and interest, as opposed to interest only payments. May also be used in a lease where the Landlord incurs costs for additional tenant improvements which are effectively treated as a debt and repaid by tenant over the term of the lease.

6.  **Appraisal**: An estimate of opinion and value based upon a factual analysis of a property by a qualified professional.

7.  **Appreciation**: Increase in value over the cost.

8.  **"As-Is" Condition**: The acceptance by the Tenant of the existing condition of the premises at the time the lease is consummated. This would include any physical defects.

9.  **Assignment**: A transfer by lessee of lessee's entire estate in the property. Distinguishable from a sublease where the sublessee acquires something less than the lessee's entire interest.

10. **Attorn**: To turn over or transfer to another money or goods. To agree to recognize a new owner of a property and to pay him/her rent. In a lease, when the Tenant agrees to attorn to the purchaser, the Landlord is given the power to subordinate tenant's interest to any first mortgage or deed of trust lien subsequently placed upon the leased premises.

11. **Balloon Payment**: A payment which after a number of years is larger & usually pays off the loan.

12. **Base Building**: The existing shell condition of a building prior to the installation of tenant improvements. This condition varies from building to building, landlord to landlord, and generally involves the level of finish above the ceiling grid.

13. **Base Rent**: A set amount used as a minimum rent in a lease with provisions for increasing rent over the term of the lease. A specific amount used either as a minimum rent in a lease (retail) which uses a percentage of sales or overage for additional rent or sets a base onto which is added expenses and taxes in a net lease or increases in those items in a fully serviced lease.

14. **Base Year**: Actual taxes and operating expenses for a specified base year, most often the year in which the lease commences.

15. **Bay**: The distance between lines of columns forming a square.

16. **BOMA**: Building Owners and Managers Association. BOMA publishes the definition of rentable and useable area, which is used to determine the square footage leased in most commercial office buildings.

17. **Building Classifications**: Building classifications in most markets refer to Class "A", "B", "C" and sometimes "D" properties. While the rating assigned to a particular building is very subjective, Class "A" properties are typically newer buildings with superior construction and finish in excellent locations with easy access, attractive to credit tenants, and which offer a multitude of amenities such as on-site management or covered parking. These buildings, of course, command the highest rental rates in their sub-market. As the "Class" of the building decreases (i.e. Class "B", "C" or "D") one component or another such as age, location or construction of the building becomes less desirable.

    Note that a Class "A" building in one-sub-market might rank lower if it were located in a distinctly different sub-market just a few miles away containing a higher end product.

18. **Building or "Core" Factor**: Represents the percentage of Net Rentable Square Feet devoted to the building's common areas (lobbies, restrooms, corridors, etc). This factor can be computed for an entire building or a single floor of a building. Also known as a Loss Factor or Rentable/Usable (R/U) Factor, it is calculated by dividing the rentable square footage by the usable square footage.

19. **Building Shell**: The skeleton of a building to which the finished exterior and interior are applied. It includes the building foundation.

20. **Building Skin**: The exterior materials that cover a building's shell.

21. **Building Standard**: A list of construction materials and finishes that represent what the Tenant Improvement (Finish) Allowance / Work Letter is designed to cover while also serving to establish the Landlord's minimum quality standards with respect to tenant finish improvements within the building. Examples of standard building items are: type and style of doors, lineal feet of partitions, quantity of lights, quality of floor covering, etc.

22. **Building Standard Plus Allowance**: The Landlord lists, in detail, the building standard materials and costs necessary to make the premises suitable for occupancy. A negotiated allowance is then provided for the Tenant to customize or upgrade materials.

23. *Build-out*: The space improvements put in place per the tenant's specifications. Takes into consideration the amount of Tenant Finish Allowance provided for in the lease agreement.

24. **Build-to-suit**: A customized design and build approach to a tenant's space usually resulting in a single occupant building which is then leased or sold to the tenant.

25. **Capital Expenses**: If something is bought for the building such as a type of pump, accounting rules say that if it is a certain type of expense it is a capital expense which means it can depreciate it over a long time, but if it is an ordinary expense it can be all expensed in the year it was purchased. Capital expenses are good for tenants and ordinary expenses is good for landlords.

26. **Certificate of Occupancy**: A document presented by a local government agency or building department certifying that a building and/or the leased premises (tenant's space), has been satisfactorily inspected and is/are in a condition suitable for occupancy.

27. **Change Order**: This is a document which contains new pricing for work the tenant wants and it causes an increase in cost, but also may cause an increase in construction time.

28. **Circulation Factor**: Interior space required for internal office circulation not accounted for in the Net Square Footage. Based upon our experience, we use a Circulation Factor of 1.25 to 1.35 is typical x the Net Square Footage for office and fixed drywall areas and a Circulation Factor of 1.45 x the Net Square Footage for open area workstations.

29. **Clear-Span Facility**: A building, most often a warehouse or parking garage, with vertical columns on the outside edges of the structure and a clear span between columns.

30. **Commencement Date**: The date on which a lease begins. This is typically but not always the day on which the tenant takes possession of the leased space, which usually occurs upon substantial completion of the tenant improvements.

31. **Commercial property**: Other than residential. Owner or leased property such as office, research, retail and industrial properties. Also includes apartment buildings as an investment.

32. **Commission**: The fee paid to a real estate broker as procuring cause and/or for his or her services rendered in a real estate transaction. May be paid by either party in a transaction; it is usually governed by a prior written agreement as to how much it will be and when it will be paid. The amount of commissions are usually driven by the market. A broker should fix a commission rate per market for your area. This should be set forth at the time a showing occurs. This needs careful documentation. A word of advice to both Landlord and Tenant, get it signed by the <u>Owner</u> and if possible the Lender.

33. **Common Area**: Common area is the area used in common by the tenants of an office building. Common area includes building and elevator lobbies, restrooms and the corridor leading from an elevator lobby to a tenant space. This includes parking lots and storage spaces.

34. **Construction Drawings**: Complete architectural drawings with notes sufficient for vendors and subcontractors to construct and for government to issue permits. Known as "CDs".

35. **Comparables**: Lease rates and terms of properties similar in size, construction quality, age, use, and typically located within the same sub-market and used as comparison properties to determine the fair market lease rate for another property with similar characteristics.

36. **Concessions**: Cash or cash equivalents expended by the Landlord in the form of rental abatement, additional tenant finish allowance, moving expenses, cabling expenses or other monies expended to influence or persuade the tenant to sign a lease.

37. **Condemnation**: The process of taking private property, without the consent of the Owner, by a governmental agency for public use through the power of eminent domain. The Owner of the taken property is paid a fair market value but that is usually his only recourse.

38. **Construction Management**: The actual construction process is overseen by a qualified construction manager who ensures that the various stages of the construction process are completed in a timely and seamless fashion, from getting the construction permit to completion of the

construction to the final walk-through of the completed leased premises with the Tenant.

39. **Contiguous Space**: (1) Multiple suites/spaces within the same building and on the same floor which can be combined and rented to a single tenant. (2) A block of space located on multiple adjoining floors in a building (i.e., a tenant leases floors 6 through 12 in a building).

40. **Contingent Fees**: Fees to be paid only in the event of a future occurrence. Examples include: Attorneys (especially in negligence cases) paid based on winning the suit and collecting damages; and a broker's commission paid only upon closing the sale of a piece of property.

41. **Contract Documents**: The complete set of drawings, specifications, bidding instructions, construction agreement, etc. used in the construction industry. The AIA (American Institute of Architects) standard forms are routinely used, but are not mandatory.

42. **Core Factor**: Represents the percentage of Net Rentable Square Feet devoted to the building's common areas (lobbies, rest rooms, corridors, etc.). This factor can be computed for an entire building or a single floor of a building. Also known as a Loss Factor or Rentable/Usable (R/U) Factor, it is calculated by dividing the rentable square footage by the usable square footage."

43. **Cost Segregation**: Cost Segregation is a lucrative tax strategy approved and endorsed by the IRS since 1997. These improved rulings allow the reclassification of specific real property assets (Section 1250) that normally receive a depreciation life of 39 years (commercial real property) or 27.5 (commercial residential) into "tangible personal property (Section 1245) that is now treated as 5, or 7 year property. Land improvements can now be treated as 15 years property for depreciation purposes. Due to these improved rulings, a percentage of the electrical, plumbing, mechanical and site improvements of a building, along with hundreds of other components can be allocated into shorter lives translating into immediate cash flow for our clients. In other words, who would you rather hold onto your money, the IRS or you? By writing off a portion of the build in the early years, you can use the accelerated deductions to offset ordinary income tax in today's dollars. (Time Value of Money).

44. **CPI**: (Consumer Price Index) A measure of inflation as determined by the US federal government using a "basket of goods". Used in leases as an impartial benchmark for the calculation of escalations and an increase in owner's invested capital.

45. **Default**: The general failure to perform a legal or contractual duty or to discharge an obligation when due. Some specific examples are: 1) Failure

to make a payment of rent when due. 2) The breach or failure to perform any of the terms of a lease agreement.

46. **Demised Area**: The walled off and secured area of a leased space, separated from spaces leased to others (by a "demising" wall). Also measured as useable area.

47. **Demising Walls**: The partition wall that separates one tenant's space from another or from the building's common area such as a public corridor.

48. **Depreciation**: This is an accounting function and allows the owner or income producing property to deduct 1/3 of the cost of the building each year.

49. **Discount Rate**: The rate of interest used in a present value analysis representing the "time value of money".

50. **Dollar Stop**: An agreed dollar amount of taxes and operating expense (expressed for the building as a whole or on a square foot basis) over which the Tenant will pay its prorated share of increases. May be applied to specific expenses (e.g. property taxes or insurance).

51. **Effective Rent**: The average per square foot rent paid by the tenant over the term of a lease. Takes into account only free rent and stepped rents. Does not include allowances, space pockets, free parking and other similar landlord concessions.

52. **Efficiency Factor**: Represents the percentage of Net Rentable Square Feet devoted to the building's common areas (lobbies, rest rooms, corridors, etc.). This factor can be computed for an entire building or a single floor of a building. Also known as a Core Factor or Rentable/Usable (R/U) Factor, it is calculated by dividing the rentable square footage by the usable square footage.

53. **Eminent Domain**: A power of the state, municipalities and private persons or corporations authorized to exercise functions of public character to acquire private property for public use by condemnation, in return for just compensation.

54. **Equity Lease**: A type of joint venture arrangement in which an Owner enters into a contract with a user who agrees to occupy a space and pay rent as a tenant, but at the same time, receives a share of the ownership benefits such as periodic cash flows, interest and cost recovery deductions, and perhaps a share of the sales proceeds.

55. **Equivalent Level Rate (ELR)**: The ELR is the flat rate per square foot that, if paid each year in nominal dollars, will equal the same total present

value as a proposed lease's variable cash flows. The ELR is calculated by discounting all cash flows to a net present value per square foot and then amortizing this lump sum amount evenly over the term of the lease on a cost per square foot basis.

56. **Escalation Clause**: A clause in a lease which provides for the rent to be increased to reflect changes in expenses paid by the Landlord such as real estate taxes, operating costs, etc. This may be accomplished by several means such as fixed periodic increases, increased tied to the Consumer Price Index or adjustments based on changes in expenses paid by the Landlord in relation to a dollar stop or base year reference.

57. **Estoppel Certificate**: A signed statement certifying that certain statements of fact are correct as of the date of the statement and can be relied upon by a third party, including a prospective lender or purchaser. In the context of a lease, a statement by a tenant identifying that the lease is in effect and certifying that no rent has been prepaid and that there are no known outstanding defaults by the Landlord (except those specified).

58. **Exclusive Agency Listing**: A written agreement between a real estate broker and a property owner in which the owner promises to pay a fee or commission to the broker if specified real property is leased during the listing period. The broker need not be the procuring cause of the lease.

59. **Exclusive Listing**: Any property where the owner has signed an agreement with a real estate broker to lease and/or sell their property. That broker has an "exclusive listing" on the owner's property.

60. **Expansion Option**: A right granted by the Landlord to the tenant whereby the tenant has the option(s) to add more space to its premises pursuant to the terms of the option(s).

61. **Expense Stop**: An agreed dollar amount of taxes and operating expense (expressed for the building as a whole or on a square foot basis) over which the Tenant will pay its prorated share of increases. May be applied to specific expenses (e.g. property taxes or insurance).

62. **Extension Option**: An agreed continuation of occupancy under the same conditions, as opposed to renewal, which implies new terms or conditions. In a lease, it is a right granted by the landlord to the tenant whereby the tenant has the option to extend the lease for an additional period of time. Usually there is some increase built into the rate for the extended term. Sometimes a Landlord will grant a tenant the right to renew his lease. In most cases there is no length stated nor rent stipulation as it is too much of a risk.

63. **Face Rental Rate**: The "asking" rental rate published by the Landlord.

64. **Fair Market Rent**: The rent which would be normally agreed upon by a willing landlord and tenant in an "arm's length transaction" for a specific property at a given time, even though the actual rent may be different. In a lease, the term "fair market rent" is defined in a number of different ways and is subject to extensive negotiation and interpretation.

65. **First Refusal Right or Right Of First Refusal (Purchase)**: A lease clause giving a Tenant the first opportunity to buy a property at the same price and on the same terms and conditions as those contained in a third party offer that the Owner has expressed a willingness to accept.

66. **Fixed Expenses**: Costs that do not change with a building's occupancy rate. They include property taxes, insurance, and some forms of building maintenance.

67. **Flex Space**: A building providing use flexibility between office, and other uses such as manufacturing, laboratory, warehouse, etc. Usually provides high bays and relocation flexibility for overhead doors and other entrances.

68. **Floor Area Ratio (FAR)**: The ratio of the gross square footage of a building to the land on which it is situated. Calculated by dividing the total square footage in the building by the square footage of land area.

69. **Floor Load Capacity**: The amount of weight a floor in a building is safely capable of sustaining, typically stated in terms of "per square foot". Locating heavy items close to the core or columns will increase capacity.

70. **Force Majeure**: A force that cannot be controlled by the parties to a contract and prevents said parties from complying with the provisions of the contract. This includes acts of God such as a flood or a hurricane or, acts of man such as a strike, fire or war.

71. **Free Rent**: A concession granted by a Landlord to a tenant whereby the tenant is excused from paying rent for a stated period during the lease term.

72. **Full Service Rent**: An all-inclusive rental rate that includes operating expenses and real estate taxes for the first year. The Tenant is generally still responsible for any increase in operating expenses over the base year amount.

73. **Gross Building Area**: The total floor area of the building measuring from the outer surface of exterior walls and windows and including all vertical penetrations (e.g. elevator shafts, etc.) and basement space.

74. **Gross Leasable Area (GLA)**: The total floor area designed for tenant occupancy and exclusive use, including basements, mezzanines, and

upper floors, and it is measured from the center line of joint partitions and from outside wall faces. GLA is that area on which tenants pay rent; it is the area that produces income.

75. **Gross Up**: An adjustment made to operating expenses to account for the occupancy level in a building. When operating expenses are "grossed up", it means that the building's variable expenses have been adjusted upwards to the level that those expenses would be incurred if the building was fully occupied (typically 95%) then when a tenant's % of the building is applied to the grossed up building he pays what he should be paying & the landlord will get his fair share.

76. **Ground Lease**: A lease of land only, (either vacant or exclusive of any buildings on it). Usually a net lease on a long term basis (30 years +). Ground rent should not be charged back to the tenant as an operating expense.

77. **Hold Over Tenant**: A Tenant who does not get out on the day the lease term is overA Tenant retaining possession of the leased premises after the expiration of a lease, usually there is a charge for this and is stipulated in the lease and normally it is double rent.

78. **Hotelling**: An alternative workspace concept where rather than having an assigned exclusive workspace, an employee accesses one space, perhaps being one of many such spaces in common with others on an as needed basis, and otherwise works outside of the office.

79. **HVAC**: Heating, Ventilation, Air Conditioning. A general term encompassing any system designed to heat and cool a building in its entirety, as opposed to a space heater.

80. **Landlord (Lessor)**: The party (usually the Owner) who gives the lease (right to possession) in return for a consideration (rent).

81. **Lease**: An agreement whereby the owner of real property (i.e. landlord/ lessor) gives the right of possession to another (i.e. tenant/lessee) for a specified period of time (i.e. term) and for a specified consideration (i.e. rent).

82. **Lease Agreement**: The formal legal document entered into between a Landlord and a Tenant to reflect the terms of the negotiations between them; that is, the lease terms have been negotiated and agreed upon, and the agreement has been reduced to writing. It constitutes the entire agreement between the parties and sets forth their basic legal rights.

83. **Lease Buyout**: The process by which a Landlord, Tenant or third party pays to extinguish the tenant's remaining lease obligation and rights under its existing lease agreement.

84.  **Lease Commencement Date**: The date usually constitutes the commencement of the term of the Lease for all purposes, whether or not the Tenant has actually taken possession so long as beneficial occupancy is possible. In reality, there could be other arrangements, such as an Early Occupancy Agreement, which have an impact on this strict definition.

85.  **Lease Term**: The specific period of time in which the Landlord grants to the Tenant the right to possession of real estate.

86.  **Leasehold Improvements**: Improvements made to the leased premises by or for a Tenant. Generally, especially in new space, part of the negotiations will include in some detail the improvements to be made in the leased premises by Landlord.

87.  **Lessee (Tenant)**: The party to whom a lease (the right to possession) is given in return for a consideration (rent).

88.  **Lessor (Landlord)**: The party (usually the owner) who gives the lease (right to possession) in return for a consideration (rent).

89.  **Letter of Attornment**: A letter from the Grantor to a Tenant, stating that a property has been sold, and directing rent to be paid to the Grantee (Buyer).

90.  **Letter of Credit**: A commitment by a bank or other person, made at the request of a customer, that the issuer will honor drafts or other demands for payment upon full compliance with the conditions specified in the letter of credit. Letters of credit are often used in place of cash deposited with the landlord in satisfying the security deposit provisions of a lease.

91.  **Letter of Intent**: A preliminary agreement stating the proposed terms for a final contract. They can be "binding" or "non-binding". This is the threshold issue in most litigation concerning letters of intent. The parties should always consult their respective legal counsel before signing any Letter of Intent.

92.  **Lien Waiver**: A waiver of mechanic's lien rights signed by a general contractor and his subcontractors.

93.  **Listing Agent**: The real estate agent hired by the property owner to lease a property on their behalf. The agent obtains a listing agreement, which calls for that agent to act on the owner's behalf as a fiduciary in leasing the property.

94.  **Listing Agreement**: An agreement between the owner of a property and a real estate broker giving the broker the authorization to attempt to sell or lease the property a certain price and terms in return for a commission, set fee or other forms of compensation.

95. **Load Factor**: In a lease, the load factor is the multiplier to a tenant's usable space that accounts for the tenant's proportionate share of the common area (restrooms, elevator lobby, mechanical rooms, etc.). The load factor is usually expressed as a percentage and ranges from a low of 5% for a full tenant to as high as 15% for a multi-tenant floor. Subtracting one (1) from the quotient of the rentable area divided by the usable area yields the Load Factor. At times confused with the "loss factor" which is the total rentable area of the full floor less the usable area divided by the rentable area. (If a full floor broken up into multiple tenancies has a usable are of 18,000 SF and a rentable area of 20,000 SF, the load factor is 11.1% and the loss factor is 10%.

96. **Long Term Lease**: In most markets, this refers to a lease whose term is at least three years from initial signing until the date of expiration or renewal option.

97. **Low Rise**: A building with fewer than 4 stories above ground level.

98. **Market Rent**: The rental income that a property would command on the open market with a Landlord and a Tenant ready and willing to consummate a lease in the ordinary course of business; indicated by the rents that Landlords were willing to accept and Tenants were willing to pay in recent lease transactions for comparable space.

99. **Master Lease**: A lease controlling subsequent leases. May cover more property than subsequent leases. For example: "A" leases an office building, containing ten offices, to "B". "B" subsequently subleases the ten offices individually. The ten subleases from "B" as sublessor are controlled by the lease from "A" to "B" (master lease).

100. **Mechanic's Lien**: A claim provided for under state statutes securing the priority of payment for the value of work and materials furnished in the construction or repair of real property.

101. **Mid-Rise**: A building with between four and eight stories above ground level although in a Central Business District, this might extend to buildings up to twenty-five stories.

102. **Month-to-Month**: A lease for a specific period of time, usually one month, which automatically renews itself for the same period of time, unless landlord or tenant provide notice to terminate.

103. **Moving allowance**: A specified dollar amount paid by the owner to cover expenses. Also known as owner's moving expense.

104. **NNN**: See "triple net" and "net lease" below.

105. **Net Absorption**: The square feet leased in a specific geographic area over a fixed period-of-time after deducting space vacated in the same area during the same period.

106. **Net Lease**: A lease in which there is a provision for the tenant to pay, in addition to rent, certain costs associated with the operation of the property. These costs may include property taxes, insurance, repairs, utilities, and maintenance. There are also "NN" (double net) and "NNN" (triple net) leases. The difference between the three is the degree to which the tenant is responsible for operating costs. (See also "Triple Net"). Today this generally indicates a lease in which the stated rent excludes the insurance, utilities, operating expenses and real estate taxes for the building. The tenant is then responsible for the payment of these costs either directly or as additional rent. Opposite of Gross or Fully Serviced Lease.

107. **Net Present Value (NPV)**: The calculation of NPV takes into account both the netting of cost and benefits **and** the time value of money. See Present Value.

108. **Net Rentable Area**: The floor area of a building that remains after the square footage represented by vertical penetrations, such as elevator shafts, etc. has been deducted. Common areas and mechanical rooms are included and there are no deductions made for necessary columns and projections of the building. (This is by the Building Owner and Manager Association—BOMA, Standard).

109. **Non-Compete Clause**: A clause that can be inserted into a lease specifying that the business of the tenant is exclusive in the property and that no other tenant operating the same or similar type of business can occupy space in the building.

    This clause benefits service-oriented businesses desiring exclusive access to the building's population (i.e. travel agent, deli, etc.)

110. **Non-disturbance**: So long as lease is not in default, its rights to occupancy under the lease will not be disturbed by the lessor or its successors or assigns.

111. **Normal Wear and Tear**: The deterioration or loss in value caused by the tenant's normal and reasonable use. In many leases the tenant is not responsible for "normal wear and tear".

112. **Occupancy Cost**: Any cost or change incurred by a tenant pursuant to its lease, such as rent, operating expense increases, parking charges, moving expenses, remodeling costs, etc. A copy of Bass Occupancy Cost Analysis is attached hereto.

113. **Operating Cost Escalation**: Although there are many variations of escalation clauses, all are intended to adjust rents by reference to external standards such as published indexes, negotiated wage levels, or expenses related to the ownership and operation of buildings. During the past thirty years, Landlords have developed the custom of separating the base rent for the occupancy of the leased premises from escalation rent. This technique enables the landlord to better ensure that the "net" rent to be received under the lease will not be reduced by the normal costs of operating and maintaining the property. The landlord's definition of Operating Expenses is likely to be broad, covering most costs of operation of the building. Most landlords pass through proper and customary charges, but in the hands of an overly aggressive landlord, these clauses can operate to impose obligations which the tenant would not willingly or knowingly accept.

114. **Operating Expenses**: The actual costs associated with operating a property including maintenance, repairs, management, utilities, taxes and insurance. A landlord's definition of operating expenses is likely to be quite broad, covering most aspects of operating the building.

115. **Operating Expense Escalation**: Although there are many variations of operating expense escalation clauses, all are intended to adjust rents by reference to external standards such as published indexes, negotiated wage levels, or expenses related to the ownership and operation of buildings.

116. **Option**: A term in a lease for the rights either tenant or landlord may have with respect to one another, usually with stipulations regarding timing of those rights.

117. **Parking Ratio**: The intent of this ratio is to provide an uniform method of expressing the amount of parking that is available at a given building. Dividing the total rentable square footage of a building by the building's total number of parking spaces provides the amount of rentable square feet per each individual parking space (expressed as 1/xxx or 1 per xxx). Dividing 1000 by the previous result provides the ratio of parking spaces available per each 1000 rentable square feet (expressed as x per 1000).

118. **Pass-Throughs**: An increase in operating expenses over the base year amount that is billed to the tenant as additional rent. See escalation.

119. **Percentage Rent**: Provides for a rent to be paid as a percentage of retail sales, usually quarterly or annually. Often coupled with a base rent.

120. **Premises**: The description of the leasehold and the specific square footage for which the parties enters into a lease. Typically the entire rentable area leased by lessee. Sometimes used to designate solely the

useable are leased by lessee, i.e. that for which the lessee has exclusive occupancy as opposed to the common areas.

121. **Present Value**: The present value is the amount that must be invested now to produce the known future value. For any sum invested at a given interest rate, the amount one would receive at the end of the period can be determined by taking the investment times one (1) plus the interest rate of the period to the power of the period. For example, if $10 is invested in an interest rate of 10% for one year, the investment would grow to $11 at the end of the year. It follows, then, that $11 one year from now is worth $10 today; that is $10 is the present value of $11.

122. **Prime Space**: This typically refers to first generation (new) space that is currently available for lease and which has never before been occupied by a tenant.

123. **Prime Tenant**: The major tenant in a building or, the major or anchor tenant in a shopping center serving to attract other, smaller tenants into adjacent space because of the customer traffic generated.

124. **Pro-Rata Share**: Percentage of building occupied by the tenant, which is usually based on the rentable or leasable square footage measurement of your space compared to the rentable or leasable square footage of the building.

125. **Punch List**: An itemized list, typically prepared by the architect or construction manager, documenting incomplete or unsatisfactory items after the contractor has notified the owner that the tenant space is substantially complete. A list of incomplete or unacceptable construction items which upon remedy and completion will usually complete the obligations of the contractor under a construction contract. Typically the Certificate of Substantial Completion will attach to it those incidental "punchlist" items which may be performed without delaying the Certificate of Occupancy.

126. **Reasonable Consent**: A standard applied in a lease (most often in a sublease clause), which limits the landlord's ability to withhold consent in its sole discretion. If a reasonable person would give consent to an action given the circumstances, so must the landlord. In the past landlords has the right to agree or not to agree to something for which the tenant is asking the landlord not to be unreasonable. Tenants have tried to get this concept as part of every lease, but the landlord does have specific reasons for some things which make sense.

127. **Renewal Option**: A clause giving a Tenant the right to extend the term of a lease, usually for a stated period of time and at a rent amount as provided for in the option language.

128. **Rent**: Consideration paid for the occupancy and use of real property. Also a general term covering any consideration (not only money). Recourse: In a loan enforcement it means the borrower is primarily liable for payment. That part of a loan which is questioned by some means probably hard cash, T-bill, etc.

129. **Rent Commencement Date**: The date on which a tenant begins paying rent. The dynamics of a marketplace will dictate whether this date coincides with the lease commencement date or if it commences months later (i.e. in a weak market, the tenant may be granted several months free rent). It will never begin before the lease commencement date.

130. **Rental Rate**: The amount of rent paid for the occupancy and use of real property. Typically stated on a per square foot per month or per year basis.

131. **Rentable Square Footage**: Rentable Square Footage equals the Usable Square Footage plus the tenant's pro rata share of the Building Common Areas, such as lobbies, public corridors and restrooms. The pro-rata share, often referred to as the Rentable/Usable (R/U) Factor, will typically fall in a range of 1.10 to 1.16, depending on the particular building. Typically, a full floor occupancy will have an R/U Factor of 1.10 while a partial floor occupancy will have an R/U Factor of 1.12 to 1.16 times the Usable Area.

132. **Rentable/Usable Ratio**: That number obtained when the Total Rentable Area in the building is divided by the Usable Area in the building. The inverse of this ratio describes the proportion of space that an occupant can expect to actually utilize/physically occupy.

133. **Rental Concession**: Concessions a landlord may offer a tenant in order to secure their tenancy. While rental abatement is one form of concession, there are many others such as: increased tenant improvement allowance, signage, lower than market rental rates and moving allowance are only a few of the many.

134. **Representation Agreement**: An agreement between the owner of a property and a real estate broker giving the broker the authorization to attempt to sell or lease the property at a certain price and terms in return for a commission, set fee or other form of compensation.

135. **Request for Proposal ("RFP")**: The formalized Request for Proposal represents a compilation of the many considerations that a tenant might have and should be customized to reflect their specific needs. Just as the building's standard form lease document represents the landlord's "wish list", the RFP serves in that same capacity for the tenant.

136. **Right of First Offer or First Opportunity**: (Typically in Expansions) A right, usually given by an owner to a tenant, which gives the tenant a first chance to buy the property or lease a portion of the property if the owner decides to sell or lease. Unlike under a Right of First Refusal, the owner is not required to have a legitimate offer, which the tenant can then match or refuse. If the tenant refuses to make an offer or if the parties cannot agree on terms, the property can then be sold or leased to a third party.

137. **Right of First Refusal**: (Typically in Expansions) A right, usually given by an owner to a tenant, which gives the tenant a first chance to buy the property or lease a portion of the property if the owner decides to sell or lease. The owner must have a legitimate offer which the tenant can match or refuse. If the tenant refuses, the property can then be sold or leased to the offerer.

138. **Right of Offset**: A specific clause in a lease where the tenant has the right to deduct from the rent certain costs which are due to the tenant from the landlord. Included may be the costs incurred by tenant to cure defaults of the landlord, after notice and failure by Landlord to cure the defaults. These are called "self help".

139. **Rules and Regulations**: Building standards that are binding on the tenants are usually set forth in a part of the lease covering such things as use of common areas, door lettering, signs, noise, odors, moving or installation of equipment, special locks, etc.

140. **Sale-leaseback**: A financing arrangement usually designed to raise capital for the property owner or obtain favorable income tax results.

141. **Second Generation**: Refers to previously occupied space that becomes available for lease, either directly from the landlord or as sublease space.

142. **Security**: Security issues are in place & more & more buildings are asking the landlord to provide all types of security. This is mostly due to "911". This means from physical barriers, mechanical, new technology, and psychological items. With the world around us being run by tenants, landlords have beefed up their security by all kinds of methods.

143. **Security Deposit**: Generally, a deposit of money by a Tenant with a landlord to secure performance of a lease.

144. **Self-Help**: When a party to a lease (for example the tenant) moves to resolve the breach of the other party (landlord) to maintain the integrity of the agreement and delivery of services whole, and without violation of the lease.

145. **Shell Space**: The interior condition of the tenant's usable square footage when it is without improvements or finishes. While existing improvements

and finishes can be removed, thus returning space in an older building to its "shell" condition, the term most commonly refers to the condition of the usable square footage after completion of the building's "shell" construction but prior to the build out of the tenant's space. Shell construction typically denotes the floor, windows, walls and roof of an enclosed premises and may include some HVAC, electrical or plumbing improvements but not demising walls or interior space partitioning. In a new multi-tenant building, the common area improvements, such as lobbies, restrooms and exit corridors may also be included in the shell construction. With a newly constructed office building, there will often be a distinction between improvements above and below the ceiling grid. In a retail project, all or a portion of the floor slab is often installed along with the tenant improvements so as to better accommodate tenant specific under-floor plumbing requirements. This usually means that the landlord of a vacant space should get the space back in a shell space condition more typically a white box.

146. **Space Plan**: A graphic representation of a tenant's space requirements, showing wall and door locations, room sizes, and sometimes includes furniture layouts. A preliminary space plan will be prepared for a prospective tenant at any number of different properties and this serves as a "test-fit" to help the tenant determine which property will best meet its requirements. When the tenant has selected a building of choice, a final space plan is prepared which speaks to all of the landlord and tenant objectives and then approved by both parties. It must be sufficiently detailed to allow an accurate estimate of the construction costs. This final space plan will often become an exhibit to any lease negotiated between the parties. This is a graphic view of how the space will look as to room size, door locations, etc. When the choice gets down to a few buildings the space planner should do a plan on all the buildings in CAD (computer assisted design) system and show all the tenant's needs

147. **Special Assessment**: Any special charge levied against real property for public improvements that benefit the assessed property.

148. **Step-Up Lease (Graded Lease)**: A lease specifying set increases in rent at set intervals during the term of the lease.

149. **Sublease**: A lease, under which the lessor is the lessee of a prior lease of the same property. The sublease may be different in terms from the original lease, but cannot contain a greater property interest. Example: "A" leases to "B" for five years. "B" may sublease to "C" for three years, but not for six years. (Rent can be greater or less than that in the prior lease.) Usually the Landlord will allow the sublease but shall want the previous tenant to be primarily responsible so fit he subtenant defaults the landlord can go after the previous tenant. Some buildings allow it and some don't. Some landlords will only allow it if they have the ability to recapture this space or receive a part of the profit if any or allow the sublease to go

through or landlord will recapture the space. All these decisions depend on the state of the market.

150. **Subordination Agreement**: As used in a lease, the tenant generally accepts the leased premises subject to any recorded mortgage or deed of trust lien and all existing recorded restrictions, and the landlord is often given the power to subordinate the tenant's interest to any first mortgage or deed of trust lien subsequently placed upon the leased premises.

151. **Substantial Completion**: Generally used in reference to the construction of tenant improvements (TIs). The tenant's premises is typically deemed to be substantially completed when all of the TIs for the premises have been completed in accordance with plans and specifications previously approved by the tenant. Sometimes used to define the commencement date of a lease.

152. **Tenant (Lessee)**: One who rents real estate from another and holds and estate by virtue of a lease.

153. **Tenant Improvements**: Improvements made to the leased premises by or for a tenant. Generally, especially in new space, part of the negotiations will include in some detail the improvements to be made in the leased premises by the landlord.

154. **Tenant Improvement ("TI") Allowance or Work Letter**: Defines the fixed amount of money contributed by the landlord toward tenant improvements. The tenant pays any of the costs that exceed this amount. Also commonly referred to as "Tenant Finish Allowance".

155. **Tenant Representation**: Arrangement whereby a prospective tenant engages a real estate broker as its exclusive agent in negotiating a lease for commercial space. Also known as a "buyer's broker".

156. **Tenant Representative**: An agent who is an advocate for the tenant. The relationship is most often the product of a signed representation agreement.

157. **Triple Net (NNN) Rent**: A lease in which the tenant pays, in addition to rent, certain costs associated with a leased property, which may include property taxes, insurance premiums, repairs, utilities, and maintenances. There are also "Net Leases" and "NN" (double net) leases, depending upon the degree to which the tenant is responsible for operating costs.

158. **Turnkey**: Referring to an owner making a property ready for a tenant to begin business by having the tenant furnish only furniture, phone and inventory, if any. Turnkey tenant improvements are provided at the landlord's expense according to plans and specifications previously agreed upon by the parties. Unlike an allowance where the tenant pays

for costs in excess of the allowance amount, the landlord bears the risk of construction in a turnkey situation.

159. **Use**: The specific purpose for which a building or space is intended to be used of for which it has been designed or arranged.

160. **Usable Square Footage**: Usable Square Footage is the area contained within the demising walls of the tenant space. Total Usable Square Footage equals the Net Square Footage x the Circulation Factor.

161. **Vacancy Factor**: The amount of gross revenue that pro forma income statements anticipate will be lost because of vacancies, often expressed as a percentage of the total rentable square footage available in a building or project.

162. **Vertical Transportation**: Elevators, stairs or escalators moving people or freight between floors in a building.

163. **Vacancy Rate**: The total amount of available space compared to the total inventory of space and expressed as a percentage. This is calculated by multiplying the vacant times 100 and then dividing it by the total inventory.

164. **Whitebox**: The interior condition of either a new or existing building or suite in which the improvements generally consist of heating/cooling with delivery systems, lighting, electrical switches and outlets, lavatories, a finished ceiling, walls that are prepped for painting, and a concrete slab floor.

165. **Workletter**: A list of the building standard items that the landlord will contribute as part of the tenant improvements. Examples of the building standard items typically identified include: style and type of doors, lineal feet of partitions, type and quantity of lights, quality of floor coverings, number of telephone and electrical outlets, etc. The Workletter often carries a dollar value but it contrasted with a fixed dollar tenant improvement allowance that can be used at the tenant's discretion.

166. **Working Drawings**: The set of plans for a building or project that comprise the contract documents that indicate the precise manner in which a project is to be built. This set of plans includes a set of specifications for the building or project.

Printed in the United States
By Bookmasters